The Causes of World War I

Stewart Ross

9403

An imprint of Hodder Children's Books

THE WORLD WARS

© 2002 White-Thomson Publishing Ltd

Produced for Hodder Wayland by
White-Thomson Publishing Ltd
2/3 St. Andrew's Place
Lewes
BN7 1UP

Series concept: Alex Woolf
Editor: Anna Lee
Designer: Simon Borrough
Map Illustrations: The Map Studio
Consultant: David Evans
Proofreader: Philippa Smith

Published in Great Britain in 2002 by Hodder Wayland, an imprint
of Hodder Children's Books.

Ross, Stewart
   The causes of World War One. – (The World Wars)
   1.World War, 1914-1918 – Causes – Juvenile literature
   I.Title II. Lee, Anna
   940.3'11

ISBN 0 7502 4020 2

Printed in Hong Kong

Hodder Children's Books
A division of Hodder Headline Limited
338 Euston Road, London NW1 3BH

Picture Acknowledgements
AKG London 4, 8, 13, 14, 16, 23,
27, 37, 40, 42(t), 47, 49, 52, 59;
Camera Press 11; Hodder Wayland
Picture Library 54; Hulton Archive
22, 26, 28, 33, 42(b), 44, 46;
Mary Evans Picture Library 12, 17,
43; Novosti 48; Peter Newark's
Military Pictures 7, 9, 10, 15, 24,
29, 31, 35, 50, 55, 58; Popperfoto
19, 20, 21, 30, 32, 34, 38, 39;
Topham Picture Point 25, 36, 45.
Cover photograph: Hulton Archive.
Archduke Franz Ferdinand and
his wife Sophie in Sarajevo,
28 June 1914.

Contents

1 A New Europe, 1871   4

2 The Great Powers, 1871-1900   6

3 The Diplomatic Revolution, 1900-07   18

4 International Rivalry, 1871-1914   28

5 The Tension Mounts, 1908-13   34

6 Sarajevo, 1914   44

7 World War, 1914-18   52

8 Whose Fault?   58

Timeline   60

Glossary   62

Sources and Resources   63

Index   64

CHAPTER ONE:
A New Europe, 1871

In the middle of the nineteenth century France was the most powerful state in continental Europe. In 1859, for example, it had twice defeated the armies of Austria, a rival power. However, only seven years later France's position was looking less secure. The new rival was Germany.

Prussian soldiers fighting in the battle of Sadowa during the Seven Weeks' War (1866).

At the time, Germany was not a single unified country, but a collection of separate states. Before 1866 Germans had been divided over two issues: first, whether the several German states might join into a single country; second, if this were to happen, which state – Prussia or Austria – would lead the unification. Then, in 1866, Prussia defeated Austria in a war that lasted just seven weeks.

The Seven Weeks' War confirmed Prussia as leader of Germany. It also brought German unification a step closer, by enlarging Prussia and putting it at the head of a powerful North German Confederation.

The war of 1866 was overshadowed by truly startling events in 1870-7. In July 1870, Otto von Bismarck, Prussia's chief minister, provoked the French Emperor Napoleon III into declaring war on Prussia. The French forces were swiftly outmanoeuvred and outfought. By September Napoleon had surrendered and Paris was under siege.

Otto von Bismarck (1815-1898)

A member of Prussia's land-owning class, Bismarck entered the Prussian parliament in 1847. He attracted attention as an anti-liberal (conservative) and was sent as Prussia's ambassador to St Petersburg and Paris. Appointed Prussia's first minister in 1862, he set about creating a united Germany with Prussia at its heart. He had achieved this aim by 1871. Thereafter, until resigning in 1890, he used his diplomatic skill to prevent the rest of Europe turning against his creation.

The German states rallied to the triumphant Prussia and, in January 1871, Emperor Wilhelm I of Prussia was declared Emperor of a united Germany. Paris surrendered ten days later. By the Treaty of Frankfurt (May 1871) France surrendered the border provinces of Alsace and Lorraine to Germany. Occupied by German troops, France also had to pay Germany 5 billion francs compensation because it had been the first to declare war.

These events overturned the European balance of power. The new Germany, proud and rich, had replaced France as the major player in continental Europe. The French, punished and humiliated, thirsted for revenge. It was a situation fraught with many dangers...

Revenge

The German seizure of Alsace and Lorraine led to France's powerful cries for revenge. As early as February 1871, for example, the writer Victor Hugo was declaring,

'The hour will sound – I can feel already the coming of that immense revenge... Then France will stand upright again! Oh! Then she will be a power to reckon with. We shall see her, at a single stroke, resume possession of Alsace, resume possession of Lorraine! Is that all? No, we shall see her ... resume possession ... of all the left bank of the Rhine as well.'

Alistair Horne, *The Fall of Paris*

This map shows the various states that made up the German Empire in 1871.

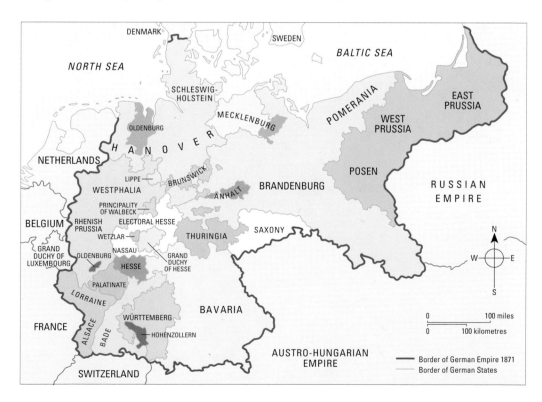

5

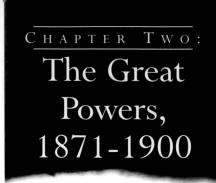

CHAPTER TWO:
The Great Powers, 1871-1900

The Roots of War

The First World War (1914-18) began as a European conflict. Only gradually did it develop into a world war. The United States, for example, was not directly involved until 1917, and the fighting had little effect on the lives of millions of South Americans, Asians and Africans. The roots of the conflict, therefore, are to be found in the European situation forty or so years before its outbreak.

There are three fundamental differences between the Europe of the later nineteenth century and the Europe of today. First, there were fewer independent countries. For example, Slovakia, Ukraine and Poland were provinces within larger empires. The existence of these European empires is the second difference – Austria (Austria-Hungary after 1867), Russia, Germany (after 1871) and Turkey were not individual countries, but empires made up of several provinces or states.

This map shows the various empires and countries that made up Europe in the late nineteenth century.

Finally, in the later nineteenth century there was no European Union. Instead of co-operating to increase their wealth and reduce the chances of war, the separate nations of Europe were in constant and dangerous competition with each other (see Chapter 4). In the end, the result of this competition was war.

The Great Powers

Later nineteenth century Europe was dominated by seven so-called 'great powers': Britain, France, Germany, Russia, Italy, Austria-Hungary and Turkey. Four of these – Britain, France, Germany and Russia – were considered greater than the others.

Britain was the most powerful country in Europe and, until at least 1900, in the entire world. The country's population soared from 20.8 million in 1850 to 37 million in 1900. Its strength and influence rested upon its wealth, overseas empire and navy. The wealth came mainly from industrial manufacture (Britain had been the home of the Industrial Revolution) and trade. The expanding British Empire, upon which the sun never set, extended from the Caribbean islands and Cape Town (South Africa) to Hong Kong and India. The Royal Navy, although not always the world's most technologically advanced, was enormous in size and power.

France industrialized later than Britain. In 1871 it was still mainly a rural, agricultural country. Its population (about 38.5 million in 1900) was not rising sharply. Nevertheless, it was a rich country with many natural resources and a growing overseas empire. It soon recovered from the defeat by Germany in 1870-71 and set about trying to win back its position as the leading continental power.

The German Empire, without overseas colonies in 1871, was the scene of enormous and rapid economic development. It had a huge population – 56.4 million in 1900 – and modern industries.

Forging ahead: a German steelworks in the 1890s. Germany's output of steel was tiny in 1850, but by 1900 it was Europe's leading steel producer.

7

Stretching from the Pacific Ocean to the Baltic Sea and containing some 126 million inhabitants (fewer than half of whom were Russians), Russia was potentially the most powerful country in Europe. Yet its industry, although developing fast, was way behind that of Britain and Germany. In 1880, for example, Russia produced 0.4 million tonnes of iron compared with Germany's 2.7 million and Britain's 7.9 million.

Austria, which combined officially with Hungary in 1867, was one of Europe's oldest and most diverse empires. (For the sake of simplicity, we will normally call Austria-Hungary just 'Austria'.) In 1900 its bureaucratic government, headed by emperor Franz Josif (ruled 1848-1916) presided over 45.5 million Austrians, Germans, Hungarians, Czechs, Croatians, Bosnians and other nationalities. Compared with Britain and Germany, its industrial output was very small.

Like Germany, in 1850 Italy had been a collection of small states. By 1870 these had united into a single monarchy with a growing population (32.5 million in 1900). Compared with the northern powers, however, Italian industry was still in its infancy.

The tragic emperor, Franz Josif (1830-1916), Emperor of Austria (1848) and King of Hungary (1867). His son committed suicide in 1889 and his wife was fatally stabbed by a terrorist in 1898.

Tension in the East

The Turkish (or 'Ottoman') Empire – the 'Sick Man of Europe' – once one of the most powerful in the world, was in serious decline by 1870. This weakness was dangerous. As the Turkish Empire crumbled, other powers sought to take its place. This produced worrying tension in the Balkans, where the governments of Russia and Austria competed to replace Turkey as the region's major power. Indeed, it was here, in the 'powder keg of Europe' (the place most likely to explode into war), that the First World War eventually started in 1914.

James Monroe (1758-1831), the US president who established the basis of European relations with the Americas for more than a century.

The USA

Beyond Europe huge stretches of land (including Africa by 1900 – see page 13) had been swallowed up by the overseas empires of the European powers. Two powerful nations stood outside this empire system: Japan and the United States of America.

Since President James Monroe set out his 'Monroe Doctrine' in 1823 (see panel), the US had avoided becoming involved in European politics. It also successfully warned European imperialists not to involve themselves in Central or South America.

Although US development was rocked by the Civil War of 1861-5, the nation soon entered a post-war boom. By 1900 the US was rapidly overtaking Britain and Germany as the world's leading industrial power. It had also dabbled in European-style imperialism. During the Spanish-American War (1898) it took over Puerto Rico and Guam. By 1902, following its success in the war, it was also in effective control of the Philippines and Cuba.

The Monroe Doctrine

In 1823 US President James Monroe outlined to Congress his famous guidelines for US foreign policy:

'[The time is] ...*proper for asserting, as a principle in which the rights and interests of the United States are involved, that the American continents ... are henceforth not to be considered as subjects for future colonization by any European powers...* [And] *Our policy in regard to Europe ... is, not to interfere in the internal concerns of any of its powers...*'

Richard Hofstadter, *Great Issues in American History*, vol.1

Japan

Having deliberately cut itself off from outside influence for centuries, in 1868 Japan set about remodelling itself as a Western-style power to protect itself from the imperialist powers. Japanese business, industry and technology made spectacular progress. In 1902 Britain considered Japan important enough to make a treaty with it. Three years later, Japan shocked the world by defeating Russia (see page 21).

Bismarck's Diplomacy

After 1871 Bismarck's aim was to preserve the new Germany he had helped create. France, of course, was the greatest threat. But France would hardly dare attack Germany without an ally. Bismarck's main task, therefore, was to keep France isolated.

Germany had little to fear from Britain. Britain was France's traditional European enemy and her main colonial rival. Moreover, Britain had been on good terms with many German states since 1714, when George of Hanover (a German state) became Great Britain's George I. Queen Victoria (reigned 1837-1901) married a German prince, Albert, and most of their children married German princes or princesses. Furthermore, Britain was preoccupied with its worldwide empire and unwilling to become too closely involved in European affairs.

Queen Victoria

Victoria (1819-1901) and her husband Albert (married 1840) (above) transformed the British monarchy into an institution that was respected and admired throughout the world. She was created Empress of India in 1877. By the time of her death, as head of the British Empire, she reigned over one in four of the world's population. Through her many children and grandchildren she was related to every important royal family in Europe. Germany's Wilhelm II, for example, was her grandson.

As Turkey was too weak to play any important part in Western Europe, Bismarck concentrated his efforts on winning round France's other potential allies, Russia, Austria and Italy. Russia was the country Bismarck feared most. A Franco-Russian alliance, he realized, would make possible an attack on Germany from both east and west at the same time.

The Dual Alliance

In 1872 Bismarck made his first move towards keeping France isolated. He persuaded Wilhelm I (Emperor of Germany), Alexander II (Tsar of Russia) and Franz Josif (Emperor of Austria) to form a League of the Three Emperors. This was a rather vague pledge to uphold monarchy. (France was a republic, not a monarchy.)

The League was followed, in 1879, by the more concrete Dual Alliance between Germany and Austria. The two countries agreed to come to each other's aid if they were attacked. The Dual Alliance lasted until 1914, when Germany and Austria (the Central Powers) entered the First World War together. As early as 1879, therefore, the battle lines of 1914 were taking shape.

The Father of Modern Germany, Otto von Bismarck (1815-1898), who once stated that great issues were decided by 'blood and iron'.

The Dual Alliance

The alliance signed with Austria on 7 October 1878 formed the cornerstone of German foreign policy for forty years:

'Article I. Should, contrary to their hope, ... one of the two Empires be attacked by Russia, [they] are bound to come to the assistance one of the other with the whole war strength of their Empires, and ... only to conclude peace together and upon mutual agreement.'

Michael Hurst, *Key Treaties for the Great Powers, 1814-1914*, vol. 2

Italy and Russia

Italy wanted to become a major naval power in the Mediterranean, where France had a powerful fleet. This enabled Bismarck to expand the Dual Alliance into a Triple Alliance (1882) by including Italy. The new ally was uneasy, however, and in 1915 Italy joined the First World War against the Central Powers (see page 54).

As we have noted (page 9), Russia and Austria were eager to replace Turkish power in the Balkans. The Dual Alliance annoyed the Russians because it gave the impression that Germany was favouring Austria above themselves. To calm Russian fears, Bismarck twice renewed the League of the Three Emperors (1881, 1884). In 1887, when the League was not renewed, Bismarck arranged a secret Reinsurance Treaty with Russia. By its terms, the two countries promised not to go to war with one another.

Reinsurance Treaty

Germany and Russia negotiated the Reinsurance Treaty in 1887. The two countries agreed to remain neutral if the other went to war. There were, however, two exceptions. First, Russia refused to promise to remain neutral if Germany attacked France. Second, Germany said it could not break the Dual Alliance and stand aside if Russia attacked Austria. The treaty, which was kept secret, fell apart after Bismarck fell from power in 1890.

A propaganda poster depicting Germany, Austria and Italy as three ladies inviting Queen Victoria to join their party — the Triple Alliance. The Queen appears disinterested.

Finally, Bismarck worked to change Germany's warlike image. In 1878, following a short war between Russia and Turkey in the Balkans, he invited the major powers to a congress in Berlin (the capital of the new Germany). Here, with Bismarck acting as an 'honest broker' (a go-between), they reached an agreement over the Balkans. Similarly, in 1884-5 Berlin was the venue for an international conference that peacefully settled disagreements over the colonization of Africa (see panel).

A French cartoon showing Bismarck dividing Africa like a cake and giving pieces to the European powers.

Scramble for Africa

For much of the nineteenth century Britain regarded the African continent almost as a private possession. But, from about 1875, France, Belgium and Germany challenged this monopoly and began carving out colonies for themselves. This fit of hasty and undignified imperialism is known as the 'Scramble for Africa'. It caused serious tensions between the European nations concerned. In 1898, for example, there was a serious crisis when British and French forces met at Fashoda on the Upper Nile. Each country was seeking to control that part of Africa.

The old world and the new: Chancellor Bismarck (left) and the young king, Wilhelm II, in 1888.

Breakdown

In 1888 the German throne passed to Emperor Wilhelm II, a man who disliked Bismarck and disapproved of his careful diplomacy. Wilhelm wanted Germany to be an undisputed world power. He and his chancellor could not work together and in 1890 Bismarck resigned. When the Reinsurance Treaty was not renewed, after nineteen years of isolation, France saw her chance.

Germany's rejection of the Reinsurance Treaty alarmed the Russians. It suggested that Russia faced hostile powers – Germany, Austria and Turkey – along its entire western and south-western border. Russian and French diplomats immediately began negotiating. By 1894 Russia and France were firm allies.

Wilhelm II (reigned 1888-1918)

Emperor Wilhelm II of Germany struggled with physical disability and felt rather overawed by his powerful grandmother, Queen Victoria. He hid his inferiority complex with a show of self-confidence. After some serious errors of judgement early in his reign, he came more and more under the influence of the military. By the time war broke out in 1914 his personal power had declined considerably and he was forced to abdicate after Germany's surrender in 1918.

Nicholas II (reigned 1894-1917)

Russia's last tsar, Nicholas II, lacked flair, brains, judgement and determination. He was, therefore, ill-suited to his inherited task. Unbending in his attachment to personal rule (autocracy), he meddled in foreign affairs in ways that infuriated his ministers (see page 21). In 1904 he let Russia blunder into an unsuccessful war with Japan. Ten years later he went into a far costlier war that destroyed his empire and led to the murder of himself and his family.

The Franco-Russian alliance would last until the outbreak of war in 1914, and beyond. In other words, by 1894 the two sides that would go to war twenty years later were already drawn up. This does not mean that war was inevitable. Far from it: the Triple Alliance and Dual Entente were intended to prevent war by making each side too strong to be attacked. Moreover, in the 1890s one of the key players in 1914, Britain, was attached to neither of the two 'armed camps'.

The doomed dynasty: Tsar Nicholas II of Russia with his wife Alexandra and their son Alexis. All three were murdered in 1918 after Russia's defeat in the First World War had sparked a communist revolution in Russia.

France and Russia drew up a draft of their entente as early as 1892. It made clear that its purpose was entirely peaceful:

'France and Russia being animated by an equal desire to preserve peace, and having no other object than to meet the necessities of a defensive war, provoked by an attack from the forces of the Triple Alliance against one or the other of them, have agreed upon the following provisions:

1. If France is attacked by Germany, or by Italy supported by Germany, Russia shall employ all her available forces to attack Germany. If Russia is attacked by Germany, or by Austria supported by Germany, France shall employ all her available forces to fight Germany.'

Gordon Martel, *The Origins of the First World War*

Britain and Europe

By the late 1890s, Britain's 'splendid isolation' – an unwillingness to become closely involved in continental Europe – was beginning to look dangerous rather than splendid. She had serious disagreements with most of the great powers.

Britain was in conflict with Russia over rival claims in oil-rich Persia (Iran). In 1898-9 France and Britain came close to war over control of Fashoda in north-east Africa. In 1898 Germany had announced plans to increase the size of its navy. Britain, which believed it had an almost God-given right to rule the waves, viewed the German move with suspicion. Wilhelm II also gave support to the South African Boers, with whom Britain was at war, 1899-1902. As a result of these conflicts, Britain was becoming increasingly involved in European politics.

Splendid Isolation

In the later nineteenth century the British called their refusal to get involved in the European alliance system 'Splendid Isolation'. There was a certain arrogance in the phrase. It implied, first, that European politics were somehow beneath Britain and, second, that it was powerful enough not to need allies anyway. Neither of these points were true. By 1900 Britain was so worried by its international isolation that it began the search for allies.

Part of the French force, led by Jean-Baptiste Marchand, that confronted the British at Fashoda on the Upper Nile.

In the 1890s Germany seemed Britain's most suitable ally in continental Europe. This was bluntly suggested by Emperor Wilhelm II:

'Without alliances, [England's] ... fate will be ultimately pressed out between Russia and the United States. With my army and your fleet that combination against us will be powerless.'

I Geiss, *German Foreign Policy, 1871-1914*

Rule Britannia! A patriotic poster showing the Royal Navy guarding the British way of life against danger from overseas.

The Situation in 1900

In 1900, although there were tensions in Europe, none of them seemed likely to lead to a major conflict. The powers of the Triple Alliance and Dual Entente roughly balanced each other, and they did not talk seriously or openly of war. In 1897 Russia and Austria had agreed to keep the situation in the Balkans as it was. Nevertheless, there were four factors that could destabilize this situation.

First, would Britain remain isolated, or, if she joined one of the armed camps, which would it be? Second, how far were Wilhelm II and his supporters in the German military prepared to go to make Germany *the* European power? Third, how secure was Russia and Austria's Balkan agreement? And fourth, when and how would France try to get revenge against Germany for 1871? Time alone would bring the answers.

Hammer or Anvil?

On 11 December 1899 the German chancellor, Prince von Bülow, explained to the German parliament (the Reichstag) why he believed a strong army and navy were essential:

'The one condition... on which alone we shall maintain our position is that we realize that without power, without a strong army and a strong navy, there can be no welfare [benefit] for us. The means of fighting the battle for existence in this world without strong armaments... have not yet been found. In the coming century the German nation will be either the hammer or the anvil.'

Gordon Martel, *The Origins of the First World War*

CHAPTER THREE:
The Diplomatic Revolution, 1900-07

The events of 1900-07 are sometimes called the 'diplomatic revolution'. This means a complete, swift and permanent change in the relationships between countries. It refers, most specifically, to the end of British isolation. This involved two changes: first, Britain becoming an ally of both France and Russia; second, growing tension between Britain and Germany. In 1900 both these changes would have been hard to predict.

China

In 1900 the attention of the European powers was focused on an empire on the other side of the world, China. Now that European imperialists had divided up Africa (see page 13), there was much talk that China would be carved up next. The French were already nibbling away at the south, the Russians in the north, and the British, Japanese, Germans and Italians in the east. In 1895, for example, the Japanese had defeated China in a limited war and seized the island of Formosa (Taiwan).

Matters came to a head in the summer of 1900, when a wave of anti-Western feeling swept through the Beijing region. This was known as the 'Boxer rebellion', after the Righteous and Harmonious Fists, a secret Chinese society that led it. An American-European force restored a degree of peace. In the meantime, Russia had occupied the northern Chinese province of Manchuria. Many thought that this would spark the partition of China.

Boxer Rebellion, 1900

For many years the Chinese had resented Western exploitation of their country. Groups such as the Society of Righteous and Harmonious Fists (the Boxers) also disliked the advances of Christianity. Discontent flared in the summer of 1900, when Chinese protestors killed Christian missionaries and seized Western embassies in Beijing. The 'rebellion' was harshly crushed by a six-nation force (Germany, France, Japan, Russia, Britain, USA) and China was asked to pay an impossible $330 million compensation.

A sentenced Boxer rebel is publicly beheaded.

Britain was tied up with a war in South Africa. Germany had few forces in the Far East. The two agreed, therefore, that the Chinese Empire should not be divided up. Their agreement was aimed at Russia, which was in the best position to move into the rest of China.

Anglo-Japanese Alliance

At this point (1901), Japan suggested an alliance with Britain. They could take care of Russia's armies in the east, if Britain dealt with Russia's ally, France. Britain would have preferred an alliance with Germany, but the Germans asked that they join the Triple Alliance. The British government refused to do this. So, on 30 January 1902, British isolation ended with the signing of the Anglo-Japanese Alliance.

The alliance said that if either Britain or Japan were attacked by two or more countries, the other would come to their aid. In practical terms, this meant that if Japan and Russia went to war over China (which was quite likely), and France joined in on the side of Russia (its ally), then Britain would have to go to war with France. The British government was greatly alarmed by the thought of having to fight a major European war because of a squabble between Japan and Russia in the Far East. Somehow, they decided, they needed to be on better terms with France.

The Entente Cordiale

The French were also nervous. They too had no wish for a European war as a result of what was happening in China. Furthermore, in 1902 the Triple Alliance was renewed for ten years. Finally, France was worried that unrest in Morocco would spill over into its colony of Algeria.

Paving the way for the entente: crowds flock to catch a glimpse of Edward VII during his state visit to Paris in 1903.

Anglo-French relations were improving when, in May 1903, King Edward VII made an official visit to Paris. The French liked the king, a portly man of the world, and greeted him with considerable affection. A return visit to London by the French president, Émile Loubet, and foreign minister, Théophile Delcassé, in July was equally successful.

Boosted by these signs of friendship, the French and British governments signed what they called an 'entente cordiale' (friendly agreement) in April 1904. The entente sorted out colonial differences – France was free to extend its influence into Morocco, for example, in return for recognizing British possession of Egypt. However, the entente was not an alliance.

The First Moroccan Crisis, 1905

After the signing of their entente cordiale with Britain, in 1905 the French sent a mission to Fez, the Moroccan capital. At this time Morocco was an independent state, but both France and Spain had much influence over what happened there. The French mission demanded that the Moroccan government reform itself. The Sultan of Morocco appealed to Germany for help, which sparked the arrival of Wilhelm II. At the Algeçiras Conference French influence in Morocco was confirmed. The part of the Moroccan coast opposite the British base at Gibraltar, however, remained under Spanish influence.

It talked of no enemy and made no plans for war. It was, nevertheless, a significant step towards a new alignment of European power.

Russian Weakness

While the British and French were negotiating their entente, war broke out in the Far East. In February 1904 Japanese forces successfully attacked the Russian base of Port Arthur in China. To the surprise of most people, Japan's first success was followed by more victories. One of the most startling occurred in May 1905. Russia's Baltic fleet sailed round the world via the Cape of Good Hope and was promptly smashed to pieces by the Japanese at Tsushima.

Seeing Russia in a weak position, the Germans suggested it might like to break with France and ally with Germany. Tsar Nicholas II and Emperor Wilhelm II signed an alliance on the Baltic island of Bjorko in July 1905. However, the tsar's advisors rejected the idea and the alliance never materialized.

Russo-Japanese War, 1904-5

This short but costly war, in which Japan defeated imperial Russia, was fought on Chinese soil and at sea. It proved to be a significant turning point in twentieth century history. Japan's victory marked its arrival as a major power. Second, the war showed up the incompetence of the Russian military command – an ominous warning of what was to happen during the First World War. Finally, Russia's defeat discredited the tsar's government and led to the 1905 Revolution. This was a foretaste of the more serious revolutions of 1917.

A new power has arisen in the East: Japanese guards with their Russian prisoners, 1905.

The Entente Tested

Meanwhile, the Germans had been trying to get at France another way. In March 1905 Emperor Wilhelm II landed at the Moroccan port of Tangier and, headed by a band, paraded through the streets. This was a deliberate threat to France, which saw Morocco as a country under French influence. Delcassé, foreign minister, did not want to back down. For a time, relations between France and Germany looked very grim.

Britain made vague promises of standing by France. Nevertheless, the French prime minister, Maurice Rouvier, did not want to risk war and Delcassé was forced to resign. This, together with the humiliating defeat of France's ally, Russia, in the Far East, left Germany dominant in continental Europe.

For a number of years, advisors to the British government had been arguing that Germany posed a serious threat to Britain. After the humiliation of France and the defeat of Russia, their worries increased. So, when a conference met in Algeçiras, Spain, to sort out the Moroccan question, the British government sided firmly with France (see page 20). Now it was the German government's time to back down. Morocco was recognized as being under the joint control of France and Spain, not Germany.

Provoking the French and testing the Entente Cordiale: Kaiser Wilhelm II in Morocco, 1905.

Berlin-Baghdad Railway

The idea for the line appeared in the later nineteenth century and work began in 1903. The project was far more important for political than transport reasons. It suggested that Germany had a special relationship with the crumbling Turkish Empire in the Middle East, and that Wilhelm II was a protector of Muslim peoples (as in Morocco). This attitude annoyed the British and the Russians, both of whom had important interests in the Middle East. The line was finally finished in 1940.

The Rising Temperature

The Algeçiras Conference was an important step on the road towards the European conflict of 1914. After the conference, the powers made fresh war plans. As a result, war became a stronger possibility.

Britain and France took their entente an important step further with top level military discussions. Britain withdrew ships from the Mediterranean (where they had been based to counter a French threat) and kept them in home waters (where they could be used against Germany). In 1907 Britain formed a special force, the British Expeditionary Force (BEF), which could cross to France at a moment's notice.

This cartoon shows the capitalist steamroller of Britain and Germany crushing Muslim Turks. In fact, the Middle East was a cause of serious tension between the two western empires.

On the other side of the Channel, the French dropped old plans for a campaign against Britain. Before this, in 1902, she had undermined the Triple Alliance by making a secret agreement with Italy. This said that the Italians would not fight France if it went to war through no fault of its own.

German reactions to Algeçiras were significant. They responded to Britain's new class of battleship, HMS *Dreadnought*, with a new Navy Law. This committed them to huge expenditure on dreadnoughts of their own (see panel). General Moltke, Count Alfred von Schlieffen's successor as Chief of the German General Staff, also changed the 1905 Schlieffen battle plan (see page 25). The new version reinforced the German armies facing France in Alsace-Lorraine and weakened the planned attack through neutral Belgium.

HMS Dreadnought, *the warship that revolutionized naval warfare.*

HMS Dreadnought

Launched in 1906, HMS *Dreadnought* could outpace all other major warships. Her armour was two inches thicker and her fire-power three times that of other battleships — at four times the distance, too. By making all other battleships out-of-date, the *Dreadnought* challenged all the world's naval commanders: build similar ships of your own, or remain a second-class power. This led, inevitably, to a massive shipbuilding programme across the world, including in Japan and the USA. It also sparked a new phase in the Anglo-German naval arms race.

Schlieffen's Plan

In 1905 Count Alfred von Schlieffen, Chief of the German General Staff, drew up a battle plan to combat France and Russia. It was based on two things: (1) Germany would be fighting France and Russia, with Britain as their ally; (2) the Russian 'steamroller' would take weeks to get going. Therefore, Schlieffen planned to keep the Russians at bay with a small force while he captured Paris with a swift attack through Holland and Belgium. He explained the thinking behind the plan thus:

'Germany must strive... first to strike down one of the allies while the other is kept occupied; but then... it must... bring a superiority of numbers to the other theatre of war, which will also destroy the other enemy.'

Schlieffen's successor, General Moltke, later weakened the plan by abandoning the attack through Holland and putting fewer troops in the force moving through Belgium.

P. Kennedy (ed.), *The War Plans of the Great Powers 1880–1914*

Count Alfred von Schlieffen (1833-1913), the German general whose famous plan for war with France dominated German military thinking for a generation.

Finally, France and Russia grew closer together as the French increased their loans for the development of Russian industry. France wanted Russia to become a major industrial power as soon as possible. This would enable it to equip itself with more and better weapons with which to challenge the Germans on the battlefield.

The two sides that went to war in 1914 were now almost in place. The one piece of the jigsaw that was missing was an understanding between Britain and Russia.

The Anglo-Russian Entente

After defeat in war, followed by a revolution at home (1905), Russia wanted a period of peace and calm. To bring this about, its foreign minister, A.P. Izvolsky, opened negotiations with Britain. The main sources of friction between the two empires were colonial squabbles, particularly in Afghanistan and Persia. These differences were sorted out in the Anglo-Russian entente of August 1907.

Sir Edward Grey, the influential British foreign secretary for ten momentous years (1906-16).

An End to Drift

Sir Edward Grey, the British foreign secretary, explained why Britain had felt it necessary to reach an entente with Russia:

'An agreement with Russia was the natural complement of the agreement with France; it was also the only practical alternative to the old policy of drift, with its continual complaints, bickerings, and dangerous frictions.'

E. Grey, *Twenty-five Years 1892-1916* vol. 1

A French propaganda poster depicting the Triple Entente (left to right: France, Russia, Britain) facing Germany.

Like the previous agreement with France, Britain's entente with Russia was not a treaty. It was simply a colonial understanding and contained no military alliance. Nevertheless, it confirmed Britain's place on the side of France and Russia, opposed to the Triple Alliance of Germany, Austria and Italy.

How Secure?

From one point of view, the formation of the Triple Entente (France, Russia and Britain) nicely balanced the Triple Alliance (Germany, Austria and Italy). The network of agreements and understandings made conflict less likely – no single country had anything clear to gain from going to war. An attack by one country would lead to many others joining in, with unpredictable results.

On the other hand, from a German point of view the situation looked rather ominous. It was precisely what Bismarck had feared all those years ago. Looking at the map of Europe, Emperor Wilhelm and his ministers felt they were surrounded by hostile powers – France, Russia and now Britain. It was as if they were being backed into a corner from which there might be only one way out – war.

Tough Talk

Britain's First Sea Lord Jackie Fisher believed – or said he believed – that the best way to keep the peace was to give the appearance of wanting war:

'If you rub it in both at home and abroad that you intend to be "first in" and hit your enemy in the belly and kick him when he's down and boil your prisoners in oil (if you take any) and torture his women and children, then people will stay clear of you'.

Stewart Ross, *Admiral Sir Francis Bridgeman*

CHAPTER FOUR

International Rivalry, 1871-1914

So far we have concentrated on Europe's leaders – the ministers, kings and emperors – and the decisions they took. However, when war came in 1914, it was ordinary men (and, in some cases, women) who joined the armed forces and fired the guns. So, while the politicians were making and unmaking treaties, what did the masses think about what was happening? And why, when war came in 1914, were most of them so willing to support their country?

'My country, right or wrong!'

In the years before the First World War, a mood of fiery nationalism (love of one's native land) swept Europe. As we have seen, people from similar cultural backgrounds, such as the Germans, forged themselves into new countries. Ethnic groups within empires, such as the

We love our country! British children caught up in the spirit of unthinking nationalism on Empire Day, 1913.

Serbs and Albanians within the Turkish Empire, fought to get their own independent countries. And in Europe's older nations, such as Britain and France, nationalism became almost a religion. Popular songs, anthems, flags, parades and newspaper articles all helped to feed this blind and dangerous nationalism. The mood spread to the US, too. Here, Senator Carl Schurz captured it best in the memorable phrase, 'My country, right or wrong!'

Nationalism cut two ways. Love of one's country easily became hatred of other countries. Politicians used this to get backing for their plans. For example, Germany's seizure of Alsace and Lorraine in 1871 made it easy to whip up anti-German feelings in France. So the French government's protest at Wilhelm II's presence in Morocco (see page 20) was backed by the French people.

France protects her flag, 1909. As today, before the outbreak of war in 1914 flags were powerful symbols of national spirit and pride.

European Rivalry

European rivalry took three major forms: imperial, commercial and military. We have already seen how imperial rivalry made Britain and France consider war with each other in 1898-9 (see page 16). The Anglo-French entente cordiale of 1904 and the Anglo-Russian entente of 1907 were designed to defuse such dangerous rivalry.

Other tensions were less easily calmed. The Russians and Japanese had fought to expand their empires in 1904-5 (see page 21). The British dreamed of a railway running over British-held land from Cape Town in South Africa to Cairo in Egypt. The German seizure of a large colony in East Africa made this dream impossible. Britain's imperialists were not amused.

Talk of War

By 1909 talk of war was widespread. In some quarters conflict was almost welcome:

'We appear to have forgotten the fundamental truth — confirmed by all history — that the warlike races inherit the earth, and that nature decrees the survival of the fittest in the never-ending struggle for existence...'

From *Blackwood's Magazine*, May, 1909, cited in Norman Angell, *The Great Illusion*

The Balkans

The Balkans was the most dangerous region of imperial rivalry, for two reasons. First, it comprised many different nationalities and cultures. It was also divided between Christians and Muslims. Second, it was of vital strategic importance to at least four great powers.

The Turks were most interested in the region – after all, in 1800 they had ruled it all. By 1900 they had largely lost control over Bosnia-Herzegovina (administered by Austria, 1878), Bulgaria (largely self-governing, 1878), Greece (independent, 1830), Montenegro (independent, 1878), Romania (independent, 1878) and Serbia (independent, 1878). The Turks now wished to hang on to Macedonia, Albania and Thrace.

Britain wanted to keep the great powers out of the Balkans. It was worried about a hostile power controlling the Eastern Mediterranean. This would threaten access to the Middle East's newly important oil wells and the Suez Canal. The canal was the direct route to India, Britain's imperial jewel.

Ships passing through the Suez Canal. The British had a special interest in the canal and surrounding areas as the waterway was a vital route to India.

Serbia

Before it was conquered by the Turks, Serbia was an independent Christian kingdom. It remained under Turkish rule until 1830, when it was given self-government. Granted full independence in 1878, it became a kingdom in 1883. King Peter I Karadordevic gave his country parliamentary government. By 1908, backed by Russia, Serbia saw itself as the chief barricade against Austria expanding further into the Balkans. This put it at the heart of the events of 1914 that led to war.

The fiercest Balkan rivalry was between Russia and Austria. They were jealous of each other's ambitions. The Russians claimed a special relationship with Slav people of Orthodox (a branch of Christianity) faith. This made it an automatic ally of the small but powerful Serbia.

Austria frowned on Balkan nationalism in case it spread north-west into its empire. It was relieved, therefore, when in 1878 it was allowed to administer Bosnia-Herzegovina by the Congress of Berlin. The decision was not appreciated by the Russians.

In 1898, Austria and Russia agreed to shelve their differences over the Balkans for the time being. The understanding defused one of the world's most dangerous flashpoints. But how long would it last?

A world-wide family of peoples: members of the British Empire welcome the ex-Boer republic of Transvaal into the British Empire (symbolized by Britannia) at the end of the Anglo-Boer War.

Nationalism and Imperialism

The Conservative politician Joseph Chamberlain loved Britain and its empire, and believed they had a key role to play in world history:

'... our object is ... the realization of the greatest ideal which has ever inspired statesmen in any country or in any age – the creation of an Empire such as the world has never seen. We have to cement the union of the states beyond the seas; we have to consolidate the British race.'

C.W. Boyd, ed., *Mr Chamberlain's Speeches*, vol. 2

Commercial Rivalry

Imperial rivalry was linked to commercial rivalry — competing in world trade. Britain's huge empire gave it a massive economic advantage. Its colonies provided cheap raw materials and commodities, like rubber and tea. Moreover, Britain was in an ideal position to sell its manufactured goods to its colonies.

By 1900, however, Britain was losing its position as the world's leading manufacturing and trading nation. It still owned half the world's merchant ships, but the USA produced more goods and Germany was forging ahead in modern industries such as electronics. Commercial rivalry did not lead to war, but it was another factor in the growing international hostility.

Military Rivalry

The 'arms race' (military rivalry) happened as countries tried to outstrip each other in the size of their armies and navies. Germany was caught in a double arms race. When Germany decided to match Britain's

The British Empire at work: Indian workers sort tea outside a factory.

HMS *Dreadnought* by building its own dreadnoughts, Britain increased its number of battleships under construction. In turn, Germany began building still more. By 1914, Britain had 34 dreadnoughts to Germany's 20.

In 1908 Russia began building up its army. In 1912, Germany increased its army by 170,000. In response, Russia launched a 'Great Military Programme' to swell its army by 500,000 men. At the same time, France extended its policy of compulsory military service (when young men had to spend time in the army or navy) from two years to three.

In 1914 the armies of the Dual Alliance totalled 1.2 million men. (Italy's allegiance to the Alliance – making it a Triple Alliance – was wearing thin. Sensibly, neither Germany nor Austria counted on Italian support.) Those of the entente powers were almost double that – and rising. The message for the Dual Alliance was obvious: if there was to be a war, the sooner it came the better.

The Arms Race

In his memoirs Sir Edward Grey, Britain's foreign secretary from 1906-16, summed up perfectly the madness of the arms race:

'One nation increases its army and makes strategic railways towards the frontiers of neighbouring countries. The second nation makes counter-strategic railways and increases its army in reply. The first nation says this is very unreasonable, because its own military preparations were only precautions, and points out ... that the first nation began the competition; and so it goes on, till the whole Continent is an armed camp covered by strategic railways.'

Grey, Viscount E., *Twenty-five Years, 1892-1916*, vol. 2

French soldiers on the eve of World War I. The soldiers' conspicuous uniforms were later changed to khaki.

CHAPTER FIVE

The Tension Mounts, 1908-13

When we talk of 'Germany' doing this, or 'Russia' doing that, we can forget that we are dealing with people. Decisions were taken not by countries but by individuals. The personalities – even the moods – of these people sometimes had a major impact on events. This was especially the case in Austria when, in 1906, Count Alois von Aehrenthal became foreign minister and General Franz von Conrad the chief of the general staff (chief military officer).

Bosnia-Herzegovina

Conrad believed Austria could survive in a dangerous world only by acting bravely and boldly. Aehrenthal was less aggressive, but he too believed that risks had to be taken. Both men had their opportunity in 1908, when a revolution changed the Turkish government.

Count Alois von Aehrenthal (1854-1912), the Austrian foreign minister whose determined action ended Russo-Austrian accord in the Balkans.

The Young Turks

The Turkish Empire – technically the 'Ottoman Empire' – had been in decline since the late seventeenth century. After 1878, opposition to the rule of old-fashioned sultans was led by a group known as the Young Turks. In 1908 and 1909 they rebelled against Sultan Abdulhamit II and forced him to resign. The new sultan, Muhammed V, promised to rule according to a constitution. It was this change of government that prompted Austria to seize Bosnia-Herzegovina.

In 1878, Vienna (the capital of Austria) had taken over the administration of Bosnia-Herzegovina because the Turkish government was thought unsuitable. Austrian ministers believed, with some justification, that the Turkish officials in the provinces were corrupt. There was no reason why the new, less tyrannical Turkish government should not now take back Bosnia-Herzegovina. Aehrenthal and Conrad were determined that this should not happen.

The majority of the inhabitants of Bosnia-Herzegovina were Serbs. If they came under Turkish rule, Aehrenthal believed, in a short time they would join with Serbia. That would make Serbia, Russia's ally, much more powerful. It would also encourage nationalist break-away movements within the Austrian Empire.

Panslavism

Panslavism – meaning 'all-Slavism' – was a Russian idea that first appeared in the early nineteenth century. It emphasized the racial and cultural links between all Slav peoples, notably the Russians and the Serbs. The movement believed that it was Russia's duty to help free all Slav peoples from the foreign rule of the Turkish and Austrian Empires. The ideas of Panslavism lingered on into the twentieth century, and provided the background to the Russian government's policy in the Balkans.

Ripping up the Balkans: Turkey (right) watches in fury as Austria seizes Bosnia-Herzegovina and Russia grabs at Bulgaria. In fact, although Austria absorbed Bosnia-Herzegovina into its empire, Russia had no more than influence over Bulgaria.

The Balkan Crisis, 1908-9

Hoping to get Russia's agreement, in September 1908 Aehrenthal met with the Russian foreign minister, Izvolsky, in Büchlau (inside the Austrian Empire). A bargain was struck: Izvolsky would accept Austria's full take-over over Bosnia-Herzegovina; Aehrenthal would support Russia's demand that its warships should be allowed to pass from the Black Sea to the Eastern Mediterranean. (This was disallowed by international treaty.)

The plan did not work. When Izvolsky returned to St Petersburg and explained his bargain, the tsar and his government turned it down. They could never agree to Bosnia-Herzegovina, with its majority Serb population, coming under Austrian rule.

Nevertheless, Austria went ahead with its annexation of the provinces. When Russia and Serbia objected, the Austrian government gave them an ultimatum: accept what had happened, or prepare for an invasion of Serbia. Germany backed its Dual Alliance partner to the hilt. Russia's friends, France and Britain, were not prepared to risk war over the issue.

Russia had no choice but to back down. Bosnia-Herzegovina remained inside the Austrian Empire.

Dummy Run

By the summer of 1909, the Vienna-St Petersburg understanding (1897) that had temporarily kept peace in the Balkans had gone for good. The Russians, humiliated and angry, were in no mood to give way a second time. France would not want to let her ally down again, either. This was not how the Germans saw things, however: they had seen the Franco-Russian alliance falter and believed it would do so again.

The Serbs were furious at the way Vienna had behaved and drew closer still to Russia. Finally, the

Alexander Izvolsky (1856-1919), the Russian foreign minister whose 1908 agreement with Austria was rejected by his own government.

Dual Alliance had stood firm. Austria felt it would be able to count on German support if it needed to get tough again.

In some ways the events of 1908-9 were a dummy run for what would happen in 1914 — except in five years time no one would be prepared to back down.

The Panther

In 1909 Britain had worked itself into a frenzy about the threat of the growing German navy. It was preparing to build eight more dreadnought-style battleships, at enormous cost. Naval expenditure was the largest single item in the British budget.

Then, two years after the Bosnia-Herzegovina crisis, trouble flared in Morocco again. The 1906 agreement had left France the major influence in Morocco, but not running the country. Taking advantage of riots against the sultan (the ruler of Morocco) in the town of Fez, in May 1909 the French sent 20,000 troops to occupy Fez.

The German government knew that they could not stop the French taking Morocco. But they decided not to let them get away with it easily. Accordingly, on 1 July 1911 the German gunboat *Panther* steamed into the Moroccan port of Agadir. It was there, the French were told, to protect German interests.

The German gunboat Panther, *sent to Morocco in 1911 as a protest against French activities there.*

Talk of War

Britain was not interested in Morocco. But it was interested in stopping the Germans from bullying the French. The British chancellor of the exchequer (chief finance minister), David Lloyd George, issued a strong warning to Germany to back off. The British fleet was made ready for action and throughout Europe people talked of war.

No war came. Germany had made its point and accepted 100,000 square miles of the Congo from France in return for recognizing France's position in Morocco. Nevertheless, it looked as if the Germans had backed down. Like the Russians in 1909, they would not want to do so again.

Lloyd George's Warning

Speaking at the Mansion House, London, on 21 July 1911, Lloyd George made it clear that Britain would not stand by and see France humiliated:

'...if a situation were to be forced upon us in which peace could only be preserved ... by allowing Britain to be treated ... as if she were of no account in the Cabinet of Nations, then I say emphatically that peace at that price would be a humiliation intolerable for a great country like ours to endure.'

H.H. Asquith, *The Genesis of War*

Peace Feelers

The 1911 Moroccan crisis worried the British government. It thought the German government was trying to use its strength to overpower France and make itself supreme in Europe. (In fact, the Germans feared encirclement by France, Russia and Britain and sought security rather than supremacy.)

David Lloyd George (1863-1945), Britain's Liberal chancellor of the exchequer whose surprisingly belligerent speech in July 1911 surprised many at home and abroad.

Lord Haldane (1856-1928), Britain's war minister whose visit to Germany in 1912 produced no agreement to end the arms race.

Consequently, in February 1912 the British war minister Haldane visited Germany to try to lower the tension between France and Germany. His main object was to end the naval arms race. The Germans agreed to do this if Britain promised to remain neutral in any future European war. This was unacceptable and Haldane came home empty-handed. From this point forward, many ministers on both sides of the Channel believed it was only a matter of time before a major European war broke out.

Italy attacks Libya

Italy was keen not to miss out on the scramble for North Africa. In September 1911 it attacked Libya, part of the Turkish Empire. Turkish resistance was not very effective.

Italy in Libya

Italy carefully prepared for its invasion of Libya in September 1911. It was allied to Germany and Austria. Britain (1902) and Russia (1909) had accepted that Italy had 'special interests' in Libya. Even so, the attack almost proved a disaster. Libya was less easily overcome than the Italians expected. Also, Conrad suggested that his Austrian forces might invade northern Italy while the Italian army was in North Africa! The idea was rejected by the Austrian government and Italy finally won control of all Libya in 1914.

The First Balkan War

Seeing the Turks brought low yet again, in March 1912 the small states of the Balkan peninsula decided it was time to drive the Turks out of the region altogether. To achieve this, Greece, Serbia, Montenegro and Bulgaria (not normally the best of friends) formed a Balkan League. In October 1912, Montenegro went to war with Turkey. The rest of the League joined in and the Turks were swiftly defeated.

Post-war Crisis

The First Balkan War made the situation in the region even more difficult than before. Neither Russia nor Austria had wanted the war. Serbia (a threat to Austria) and Bulgaria (a threat to Russia) were both bigger and more powerful than ever. To try and sort matters out peacefully, the great powers met with Balkan leaders in London in December 1912.

After months of wrangling, the Treaty of London was signed in May 1913. It left Serbia and Bulgaria larger and created the newly independent country of Albania. Unfortunately, Bulgaria had been persuaded to give up more territory than it had wanted. It felt cheated and in June 1913 war broke out again.

The Second Balkan War

It would have been better for Bulgaria if it had kept quiet. Faced by Serbia, Greece, Montenegro, Romania and Turkey, it was crushed. The Second Balkan War was ended by the Treaties of Bucharest (August 1913) and Constantinople (September 1913). Bulgaria lost territory to Serbia, Greece, Romania and Turkey.

A sign of things to come: a battlefield during the First Balkan War, 1912.

This map shows the land lost and gained by Balkan countries in 1913.

By the end of 1913, the situation in the Balkans was dangerously unstable. Serbia had doubled in size but still had no access to the sea. This meant all its supplies from abroad had to come through neighbouring states. Moreover, many Serbs felt it was their duty to 'liberate' the Serbs within the Austrian Empire. For its part, Austria was eager to attack Serbia and break it up.

During the 1913 crisis, Austria had once more threatened to attack Serbia. The Russians had not been prepared to risk war over the issue and it passed. They were unlikely to be so yielding the next time.

Austria and Serbia

Conrad, the Austrian chief of staff, made it quite clear in 1914 that he wanted Serbia brought under the control of Vienna:

'The unification of the South Slav race is one of the powerful national movements which can neither be ignored nor kept down. The question can only be, whether unification will take place within the boundaries of the Monarchy [Austria-Hungary] – that is at the expense of Serbia's independence – or under Serbia's leadership at the expense of the Monarchy ... The loss of territory and prestige would relegate the Monarchy to the status of a small power.'

Ruth Henig, *The Origins of the First World War*

Ready for action: German submarines (U-boats) in 1914. When the war came, U-boats proved more effective than surface ships in blockading British ports.

Was War Inevitable?

Nothing in history is inevitable. Nevertheless, by the beginning of 1914 it was most likely that a major conflict would be sparked by events in the Balkans.

During the previous ten years most of the great powers had been obliged to back down in crisis situations. This made them less likely to do so in future. Conrad and his staff in the Austrian military headquarters wanted war with Serbia, even if it led to a wider conflict.

Russian cavalry, outside the Tsar's Winter Palace in St Petersburg in 1914. Although a magnificent sight, Russia's huge cavalry strength proved powerless against German machine guns, rifles and artillery.

More worrying, Wilhelm II and many in the German military believed that war was bound to come, and they were preparing for it. Indeed, because the Russian army was growing so fast, they wanted war sooner rather than later. Britain had made it clear that it would fight to prevent Germany dominating Europe.

All this took place against a background of scare stories, nationalistic parades, threats and boasting. 'We are bound to win' was the cry on everyone's lips. Only a few were brave or wise enough to point out that twentieth century warfare would be different. Unlike previous conflicts, everyone would be on the losing side.

War Inevitable?

Sir Edward Grey, the British foreign secretary, outlined the position in which he thought war would become inevitable:

'Austria has determined that if Albania ceased to be Turkish territory it should not pass into the hands ... of Serbia. Serbia, borne on the tide of her own victories, might easily reach the point of inevitable conflict with Austria. If this happened, and if Russia felt that she was required to support Serbia, European war was inevitable.'

Grey, Viscount E., *Twenty-five Years, 1892-1916*, vol. 2

A French cartoon mocking Britain's fear of the latest naval and aerial warfare. In time, however, the fears were justified.

Archduke Franz Ferdinand

Another key character now stepped into the limelight. He was Archduke Franz Ferdinand, the heir to the thrones of Austria and Hungary. He was a tough, cold man with little sympathy for nationalists – like the Serbs of Bosnia-Herzegovina – who wished to leave his uncle's empire.

In the summer of 1914, Franz Ferdinand, accompanied by his wife Sophie, paid a state visit to Bosnia. This was a brave but dangerous gesture. Bosnia, fully part of the Austrian Empire for only six years, was a hotbed of nationalist terrorists. The royal family had first-hand experience of terrorism, too – the Austrian Emperor Franz-Josif's wife, Elizabeth, had been assassinated in Geneva in 1898.

Sarajevo

After watching army manoeuvres, on Sunday 28 June the archduke visited the Bosnian town of Sarajevo. It was the anniversary of the Battle of Kosovo (1389), one of the most memorable dates in Serb history. Sarajevo was only eighty kilometres from the Serbian border. The nationalist Black Hand gang had heard of the archduke's visit and prepared to ambush him.

Welcome to Sarajevo: the mayor of the city greets Archduke Franz Ferdinand of Austria and his wife Sophie, 10 am, 28 June 1914. The couple's assassination a few hours later sparked the train of events that led directly to world war.

Franz Ferdinand and Sophie arrived in Sarajevo by train and were taken by car towards the town hall. Shortly after 10 am that morning, as they were passing beside the river, a terrorist threw a bomb at the royal couple's car. Quickly, the archduke pushed it aside. It went off under the following car, causing serious injuries. Having failed in their assassination attempt, the Black Hand Gang scattered.

Assassination

After his meeting at the town hall, Franz Ferdinand asked to be taken to the local hospital to visit those injured by the bomb. On the way, his driver took a wrong turning into a side street. Quite by chance, Gavrilo Princip, a young member of the Black Hand Gang, was standing by the street corner wondering what to do.

The archduke's car stopped and began to reverse out of the side street. Hardly able to believe his good luck, Princip stepped forward and fired two fateful shots at point blank range. Franz Ferdinand and Sophie were rushed to hospital where they both died a few minutes later.

Terrorist or freedom fighter? The man who started a world war, the fanatical Bosnian nationalist Gavrilo Princip.

Gavrilo Princip (1895-1918)

Born in Bosnia, from a young age Princip devoted himself to freeing his native land from Austrian rule. He was one of six young men recruited into the Black Hand Gang by its Sarajevo leader, Danilo Ilic, specially for the visit of Archduke Franz Ferdinand. After assassinating the archduke, Princip took poison. It did not work. He was arrested and held in an Austrian prison until 1918, when he died of tuberculosis.

The Blank Cheque

The assassination of Franz Ferdinand and his wife was one of the most important events of modern world history. It started a chain reaction of events that led directly to a war that shaped the course of the twentieth century.

Austrian agents were soon on the trail of the Black Hand Gang. They learned that it was made up of Bosnian Serbs armed with Serbian weapons. Furthermore, Serbian officials had known of the assassination plot and not warned the Austrians.

Bethmann Hollweg, the German chancellor who did not believe Russia would risk war with Germany as the result of a terrorist assassination. He was tragically wrong.

This evidence gave Emperor Franz Josif just the excuse he needed. Austrian forces would attack Serbia immediately and absorb it into the Austro-Hungarian Empire. Germany, Austria's ally, believed Russia could not possibly stand by Serbia after what had happened. Consequently, the German government offered to back Austria in whatever it decided to do – a 'blank cheque' of support.

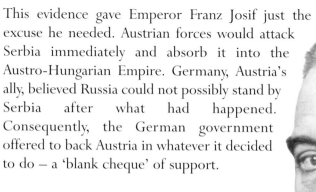

Theobald von Bethmann Hollweg (1856-1921)

Bethmann Hollweg, the German chancellor from 1909 to 1917, was not a warlike man. In 1909 and 1911 he tried to negotiate a reduction in naval armaments with Britain. He also worked hard to prevent the Balkan Wars (1912-13) spreading outside the region. However, on 5 July 1914 he made the fatal mistake of agreeing with Wilhelm II that Germany would support an Austrian attack on Serbia (the 'blank cheque'). His later warnings to Austria and Russia came too late to prevent disaster.

The Ultimatum

Things did not work out quite as the Germans expected. Unwilling to be seen as the aggressor, the Austrians did not attack Serbia immediately. Instead, after much discussion, they gave the Serbian government a list of demands that would be almost impossible to accept. This ultimatum was sent on 23 July, almost a month after the assassination.

When Wilhelm had given his 'blank cheque', he had assumed Austria would attack Serbia at once. The delay made things a lot more awkward. Russia, in particular, was given time to think things through.

Taking Sides

Russia had failed to support Serbia strongly in the past. If Austria had launched a surprise attack on Serbia, it would not have been able to do much this time, either. However, the longer the Austrians delayed, the tougher the Russian position became. If they did not now take a strong stance, they concluded, they would lose face and be seen as a second-rate power. They made it clear, therefore, that if war broke out, Serbia would not stand alone.

France, too, was in a tricky position. In 1908-9, France had failed to give Russia enthusiastic backing. It feared that if it let down its ally again, Russia might cancel its alliance with France. As a result, the French government gave Russia its support. Of all the major powers, only Britain failed to take a positive position. Some argue that this was a mistake: if Britain had urged the Russians to back off, a wider war might have been avoided.

Russian and Serbian troops, 1914. Many Russians felt a deep attachment for their 'Slav brothers' in Serbia.

Austria's Ultimatum to Serbia

The clause in the ultimatum that the Serbian government could never agree to was the fourth:

'...*to remove from military service and from the administration all officers and officials who are guilty of having taken part in the propaganda against Austria-Hungary, whose names and proofs of whose guilt the ... Royal Government* [of Austria-Hungary] *will communicate to the Royal Government of Serbia.*'

Geiss, *July 1914. Selected Documents*

Your country needs you: Russian peasants are enlisted into the army, 1914. As in most European countries, in Russia the outbreak of war was greeted with an outburst of patriotic optimism.

First Shots

On 27 July the Serbian government replied to the Austrian ultimatum. It could accept eight of the ten demands but would not agree to Austria helping choose their army officers or the ministers in their government. This was not good enough for the Austrians. They declared war on Serbia on 28 July and immediately sent in their army.

The Russians still held back. Instead of declaring war on Austria, on 30 July they mobilized their forces for action. This was a way of warning Austria to lay off Serbia. Attention now shifts away from the Balkans to Germany.

Enter Germany

The German government was sure there would be a major war. As we have seen, their military thinking was based around the Schlieffen Plan (see page 25). This meant striking first with a sudden and swift attack on France.

So as not to lose the advantage, on 31 July the German government mobilized its forces and told the Russians to stop their military preparations at once. The Russians did not reply. On 1 August 1914, Germany declared war on Russia. This crucial step made a peaceful settlement of the crisis impossible.

Long live the Kaiser! Wealthy young Germans flock to join the army, August 1914.

General Mobilization

Germany declared war on Russia because it had mobilized its forces for war. But according to the Russian foreign minister, Sazonov, his forces had mobilized against the threat of Germany:

'*... in view of the small probability of avoiding a war with Germany, it was indispensable to prepare for it in every way in good time, and ... therefore the risk could not be accepted of delaying a general mobilization now. [The tsar] ...authorised the taking of steps accordingly.*'

Ruth Henig, *The Origins of the First World War*

Belgium is ours, now for Paris! German troops on parade in Brussels, August 1914.

France and Britain

The Germans now put France into an impossible corner. If it remained neutral, they said, it must put the forts along its eastern frontier into German hands. The French refused and mobilized their forces. Germany declared war on France on 3 August and put the Schlieffen Plan into operation.

On 4 August German forces were pouring into Belgium. By a 75-year-old treaty Britain guaranteed that Belgium and Luxembourg would remain neutral. The German attack broke this neutrality. So, on 4 August, Britain gave Germany an ultimatum: leave Belgium or face war with Britain. When Britain had received no reply to this ultimatum by midnight, it declared war on Germany.

In the week since 28 July the position of the British government had changed. At the beginning of the crisis, it had stood cautiously to one side. However, by

The Scrap of Paper

Belgium became an independent country in 1830. In 1839 Britain guaranteed its independence at the Treaty of London. Sixty-five years later, when Germany was preparing its war plans against France, it looked for a way of avoiding the massive forts along France's eastern frontier. The answer, it decided, was an attack through Belgium. Although this might anger Britain, Chancellor von Hollwegg said he was sure Britain would not go to war for the sake of a 'scrap of paper' (the Treaty of London).

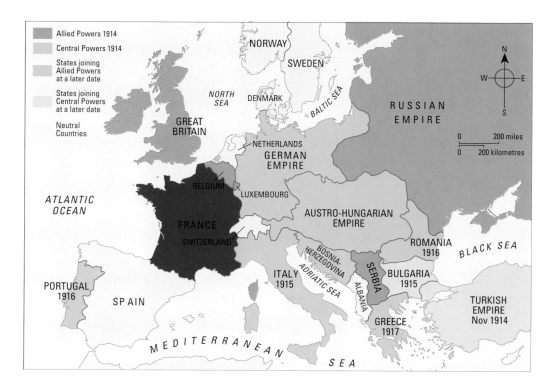

Allied Powers 1914

Central Powers 1914

States joining Allied Powers at a later date

States joining Central Powers at a later date

Neutral Countries

4 August it realized that neutrality was no longer possible. The question of Belgian neutrality was more an excuse for action than a reason.

This map shows which countries joined the Central Powers and which joined the Allied forces during the course of the war.

The War Spreads

When the Sarajevo crisis blew up, the Italian government made it clear that it would remain neutral. It did not join the war until the following year (see page 54). Other nations were less hesitant.

Montenegro joined in straight away on the side of its neighbour, Serbia. Japan, eager to get its hands on German colonies in the Far East, joined the war on Britain's side on 23 August. In November, the Turks, whose record in recent wars was dismal, sided with the Central Powers (Germany and Austria).

By December 1914 the war had spread right across Europe and beyond. Moreover, although in August many had predicted that it would be 'over by Christmas', it had hardly started.

CHAPTER SEVEN

World War, 1914-18

The war that started in the summer of 1914 was not a world war. It was known first as the 'European War', then as the 'Great War'. Finally, after the entry of the USA in 1917 (see page 57), it gradually became known as the World War. From the first, however, because Japan and the European empires were involved, the fighting was not just confined to Europe.

Imperial War

In 1914 the Japanese seized the German Pacific Islands (the Mariana, Caroline and Marshall Islands, and parts of Samoa and Papua) and helped Britain take the German base of Tsingtao in China. Turkey's entry into the war spread the conflict into the Middle East, where the British supported an Arab revolt against the Turks. The heaviest fighting took place in Gallipoli 1915-16, when the Allies failed to seize the Dardanelles.

In Africa, an Anglo-French force took German Togo (1914) and campaigns began against German East Africa (Tanzania) and German South-West Africa (Namibia). An Anglo-Nigerian army captured Cameroon, another German colony, in 1915-16. As well as fighting in the colonies, hundreds of thousands of Indians, Africans (both north and south), South-East Asians, Canadians, Australians and New Zealanders came to Europe to fight alongside the British and French.

The Arab Revolt

Eager to find new allies, in 1915 the British approached the Sherif of Mecca in Turkish-occupied Arabia. The Arabs agreed to rise up against the Turks. In return, Britain agreed to support Arab independence after the war. The revolt began in June 1916. By October 1918 Anglo-Arab forces were in Damascus and Turkish power in the Arab world was finished. To the Arabs' dismay, Britain did not support their independence movements after the war.

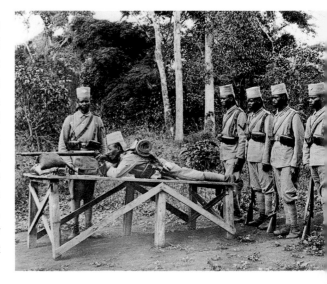

African soldiers in German South-West Africa (now Namibia) are trained to fight against British forces from neighbouring South Africa.

German East Africa, 1914-18

The campaign in East Africa (a colony about the same size as France) was one of the most fascinating of the whole world war. For four years some 350,000 soldiers of the British Empire struggled to contain 14,000 Germans and Africans. The fighting took place at sea, on land and on Lakes Victoria, Tanganyika and Nyasa. Its most memorable feature was the brilliant leadership of the German commander, General Paul von Lettow-Vorbeck, who kept the Allies at bay until almost the end of the war.

The War at Sea

The naval war was also wide-ranging. Fighting spread from the North Sea (Battle of Jutland, 1916) to South America (Battles of Coronel and Falkland Islands, 1914). Surface and submarine raiders also operated widely, but particularly in the North Atlantic (see page 56).

This map shows the locations of major naval battles during World War I.

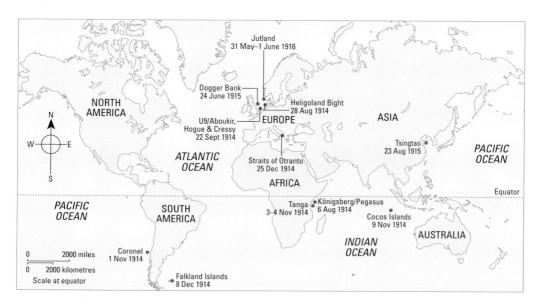

Taking Sides

Italy was in a tricky position in August 1914. Officially part of the Triple Alliance, it was pledged to join with Germany and Austria. Nevertheless, it had just fought a difficult campaign in Libya. Most Italians did not want another war. The Italian government was worried that British and French fleets would wreak havoc on the long Italian coastline.

Italy remained neutral, therefore, wooed by both sides. The Allies eventually won its support by promising those areas of the Tyrol and the Adriatic coast inhabited by Italian-speakers (Treaty of London, May 1915). Even so, the war was not widely popular in Italy.

Few Balkan states joined the war in 1914. Bulgaria, humiliated in the Second Balkan War, waited until 1915 before joining the Central Powers. Romania, Bulgaria's hostile neighbour, sided with the Allies a year later. Greece was one of eleven other countries that had joined the Allies by November 1918. By now, with Portugal, Brazil and the USA involved, the war had become truly worldwide.

American Neutrality

By 1914 America had stuck to the Monroe Doctrine for close on a century (see page 9). The outbreak of a major European war was no reason to change this. Indeed, many Americans wanted nothing to do with the problems of Europe. The victor of the 1912 presidential election, Woodrow Wilson, reflected this mood of neutrality.

War in the Alps. Italian troops moving forward to take up positions against the Austrians.

From the start, powerful sections of American society challenged the policy of neutrality. They included the wealthy families of the East Coast, who had strong links with Britain, and the majority of newspapers. It was America's duty, they argued, to side with British and French democracy against German aggression. Wilson disregarded these voices. He tried to act as a peacemaker between the two warring sides and in 1916 was re-elected under the slogan, 'He Kept Us Out Of War'.

Wilson's Neutrality

On 19 August 1914 President Wilson sent a message to all Americans in which he urged neutrality towards the European war that had just begun:

'I venture, therefore, my fellow countrymen, to speak a solemn word of warning to you against that deepest, most subtle, most essential breach of neutrality which may spring out of partisanship, out of passionately taking sides. The United States must be neutral in fact as well as in name during these days that are to try men's souls.'

Richard Hofstadter, *Great Issues in American History*

The great idealist: President Woodrow Wilson (1856-1924) who tried to keep Americans out of World War I and then, when they joined in, declared that they were on a 'crusade for democracy'.

Irritations and Anxieties

By Christmas 1916 American neutrality was coming under pressure. The American military wanted an Allied victory. Only Britain, they argued, could guarantee to keep the world's shipping lanes open for US vessels. At the same time, the US had invested huge sums in Allied countries. Its trade with them had increased six-fold since 1914. As a result, victory for the Central Powers would mean serious economic hardship in the US.

More serious was the effect the naval war was having on America. The Allies and the Central Powers were trying to cut off each other's supplies of food and materials by means of naval blockades. The British navy used mines (whose positions were known to neutrals) and surface ships. Only rarely did these tactics involve fighting or loss of life. In contrast, the Germans relied largely on submarines.

Submarine Warfare

In the first months of the war German submarines (U-boats) attacked merchant ships as follows: they rose to the surface, warned the crew to abandon ship, then sank their target with gunfire or a torpedo. The trouble was, submarines on the surface were very vulnerable to attack.

So in February 1915 the U-boats changed tactics. From now on any ship even suspected of trading with the Allies would be sunk without warning. An American tanker was sunk. Then, on 7 May 1915 a U-boat torpedoed the British liner *Lusitania* off the coast of Ireland. The liner was bound for Southampton, England, from New York. 1153 lives were lost, including 128 Americans. The news of this sinking, and of that of the liner *Arabic* (also

The Lusitania

The sinking of the *Lusitania* helped turn American public opinion against Germany. The Germans said that the liner might be targeted, but it took no action to avoid attack and was sunk in 20 minutes by two torpedoes fired by U20 on 7 May 1915. The Germans claimed that the *Lusitania* carried troops and guns and therefore was a legitimate target. The British denied these claims and their denials were believed by most Americans then and since.

The torpedoing of the Lusitania, *1915, an event that helped turn US public opinion against Germany.*

Crusade for Democracy

President Wilson led the US into the First World War with great reluctance. On the day war was declared, he justified the action by claiming that US forces would help spread democracy around the world:

'We have no selfish ends to serve. We desire no conquest, no dominion. We seek no indemnities for ourselves, no material compensation for the sacrifices we shall freely make. We are but one of the champions of the rights of mankind … The world must be made safe for democracy.'

Richard Hofstadter, *Great Issues in American History*, vol. 2

with Americans on board), swung US public opinion strongly against Germany. Worried that the US might enter the war against them, the Germans ended unrestricted submarine warfare four months later.

America Goes to War

After the sinking the American public took a greater interest in the war. On 19 January 1917 the German foreign minister, Arthur Zimmermann, sent a secret message to a German diplomat in Mexico. It announced that Germany planned to reintroduce its U-boat 'sink at sight' tactic on 1 February 1917. Zimmermann also suggested that if Mexico joined the Central Powers, it might take over part of the southern USA. He also hinted that if Japan joined the Central Powers, it would be invited to attack US naval bases in the Pacific.

The British intercepted the telegram and passed it on to the US government. When the press was told of its contents, war fever gripped the US. A month later (6 April 1917), America formally declared war on Germany.

CHAPTER EIGHT

Whose Fault?

The causes of World War I may be summarized in three parts. The first two are the long-term causes, or background to the war. The third is the immediate cause, or trigger.

- One: in an age of nationalism, the great European powers found themselves in a spiral of colonial, commercial and military rivalry for the domination of Europe.
- Two: fearing for their security, the powers set up networks of alliances; these made a limited war almost impossible.
- Three: Franz Ferdinand's assassination sparked a crisis between Austria and Russia in which neither would back down; the war that followed was spread over the continent and beyond by the alliance system.

French soldiers in the Argonne, 1915. The horror of the trench warfare made it almost impossible for the victors to forgive or forget.

Anyone to Blame?

This simple summary ignores millions of crucial details: the personalities of the people in power, for example, the decisions they took – and chance. How different would history be, for instance, if the archduke's driver had not taken a wrong turning off Appel Quay, Sarajevo, at 10.45 am on Sunday 28 June 1914? In other words, was World War I caused by a careless chauffeur? After the war, when the victors met at Versailles to work out a peace settlement, they wanted someone to blame for the unspeakable horrors they had just witnessed. They blamed not the Sarajevo chauffeur but the entire German nation. Germany was blamed more than Austria because the Germans had caused the most damage in Western Europe, and also because they had turned the Austro-Serbian squabble into a European war. Germany, they claimed, had sought war, planned for war and finally declared war.

Although these observations were, in part, true, they were only one aspect of the story. Why was Germany in a position where it thought war the only option? Moreover, in all countries, from Serbia to Britain, there were those who sought and planned for war. In the end, perhaps responsibility for the war lay not with Germany but with the European system of alliances, threats and naked rivalry. After so much talk of war for so long, it was not surprising that it eventually broke out.

The Treaty of Versailles

The fate of Germany was settled at the Treaty of Versailles, 1919. France and, to a lesser extent, Britain called for revenge and for compensation for the losses they had suffered. President Wilson attended, but the United States senate refused to endorse the agreement. As a result, Germany was blamed for causing the war, lost territory, was banned from having effective armed forces and asked to pay 226 billion gold marks. These terms echoed the harsh terms imposed on France in 1871. As in 1871, they were no basis for a long-term settlement – and the Second World War broke out in Europe only 20 years later.

Clemenceau (left), Wilson (centre) and Lloyd George (far right) at the Versailles peace conference, 1919. The treaty they negotiated proved no more than a 20-year cease-fire.

Timeline

1815 End of the Napoleonic Wars. German Confederation formed of most of the states within the German geographical area.

1819 German Customs Union formed.

1830 Greece independent from the Turkish Empire.

1839 Treaty of London guarantees the neutrality of Belgium.

1854-6 Crimean War between Russia and Britain. (Ends with the Treaty of Paris.)

1859-70 Kingdom of Italy created.

1861 Romania formed.

1866 **June-July** Prussia and Austria go to war. Austria is defeated in seven weeks.

1870-71 Franco-Prussian War.

1871 **January** German Empire proclaimed at Versailles in France.
May Treaty of Paris. France gives up Alsace and Lorraine to Germany.

1872 League of Three Emperors formed between emperors of Germany, Austria-Hungary and Russia.

1877-8 Russo-Turkish War.

1878 Congress of Berlin. Serbia, Bosnia-Herzegovina, Bulgaria, Montenegro and Romania achieve varying degrees of independence from Turkey.

1879 Austro-German Dual Alliance.

1888 League of Three Emperors renewed.

1882 Italy forms Triple Alliance with Germany and Austria-Hungary.

1887 League of Three Emperors expires.
Russo-German Reinsurance Treaty.

1888 Wilhelm II becomes emperor of Germany.

1890 **March** Bismarck resigns as Prussia's chief minister.
June Reinsurance Treaty between Russia and Germany not renewed.

1891 France and Russia begin negotiations for a military alliance.

1894 French and Russian Alliance signed.

1897 Austro-Russian agreement over Balkans.

1898 Fashoda crisis between Britain and France on the Upper Nile in North Africa. First German Navy Law.

1899-1902 Anglo-Boer War in South Africa.

1900 Second German Navy Law increases the size of the German navy.
Boxer Rebellion in China.

1902 Anglo-Japanese Alliance. Secret treaty between France and Italy.

1904 Anglo-French entente cordiale.
Russo-Japanese War (to 1905).

1905 Schlieffen Plan drawn up. Revolution in Russia overthrows Tsar Nicholas II. First Moroccan crisis as Germany seeks to limit French influence in Morocco.

1906 **January-April** Algeçiras Conference ends the Moroccan crisis when Germany backs down.
HMS *Dreadnought* launched by the British Navy.

New German Navy Law plans a massive programme of battleship building.

1907 British Expeditionary Force formed.
Anglo-Russian entente.

1908 **September** Russian and Austrian foreign ministers agree at Büchlau not to upset the situation in the Balkans.
October Büchlau agreement falls apart.
Austria-Hungary annexes Bosnia and Herzegovina.
Russia backs down.

1911 Second Moroccan crisis as Germany again seeks to limit French influence in the country.
21 July Lloyd George's Mansion House speech.
October Italy invades Libya.

1912 **February** British War Minister Haldane visits Berlin.
May Serbia, Montenegro, Bulgaria and Greece form the Balkan League.
October Balkan League defeats Turkey in First Balkan War (to 1913).

1913 **June-August** Bulgaria crushed in Second Balkan War.

1914 **January** German officer takes command of the Constantinople garrison in the Dardanelles.
28 June Archduke Franz Ferdinand assassinated in Sarajevo, Bosnia.
23 July Austrian ultimatum to Serbia.
27 July Serbia's reply to the ultimatum rejected by Austria.

28 July Austria declares war on Serbia.
30 July Russia begins to mobilize troops.
31 July Germany's ultimatum to Russia.
1 August Germany declares war on Russia.
France mobilizes troops.
3 August Germany declares war on France.
4 August German troops enter Belgium.
Britain's ultimatum to Germany.
(Midnight) Britain at war with Germany.
12 August Britain and France declare war on Austria.
23 August Japan joins Allies.
November Turkey joins Central Powers.

1915 **February** Germany begins unrestricted submarine warfare.
May Italy joins Allies.
September Bulgaria joins Central Powers.

1916 **August** Romania joins Allies.

1917 **January** Zimmermann telegram.
Germans reintroduce unrestricted submarine warfare.
6 April USA declares war on Germany.

1918 **11 November** End of First World War.

1919 **January** Paris Peace Conference opens.
June Treaty of Versailles signed.

Glossary

aggressor person or state that starts a conflict.

alliance agreement between states for their mutual help in time of war.

Allies Russia, France, Britain, Italy, the USA and the countries that fought with them in the First World War.

annex to take over.

armaments weapons of all kinds, from rifles to warships.

assassinate to murder a well-known figure, usually for political reasons.

Austria-Hungary dual Monarchy of Austria and Hungary, joined in 1867. In this book the Dual Monarchy is called simply 'Austria'.

Balkans region between the Black Sea and the Adriatic.

blockade cutting off supplies.

Bosporus small sea between the Black Sea and the Aegean.

bureaucracy civil service (literally, 'rule by office holders').

bureaucratic government government in which officials have a great deal of power.

Central Powers Germany, Austria-Hungary and Turkey.

chief of staff top military commander.

colony a country ruled by an overseas empire.

conference high level meeting.

Continental Europe Europe apart from the offshore islands, such as Britain and Cyprus.

congress a major meeting of delegates from various groups or nations.

Dardanelles narrow strip of water between the Bosporus and the Aegean, separating Western Turkey from Asian Turkey.

democracy government by the people or their elected representatives.

diplomacy high-level contacts between states.

dreadnought fast, heavily armoured battleship, after HMS *Dreadnought* (launched in 1906).

economy finances, services and industry of a state or empire.

empire many territories, sometimes in different parts of the world, under the same government.

entente an understanding or agreement, usually between nations.

exports goods shipped for sale abroad.

foreign policy a state's policy towards other states.

foreign secretary minister responsible for relations with other countries.

garrison troops in a regular base.

Imperial relating to an empire.

imports goods shipped into a country from abroad.

Industrial Revolution swift change that began in the later eighteenth century and which saw the introduction of large scale manufacture in factories using powered machines.

liberal generous, broad-minded, open.

limited war war in which one or both sides do not use all their resources.

liner ocean going passenger ship.

merchant ship ship for carrying cargo.

military, the armed forces.

mine a bomb hidden underwater or under soil.

mobilize to prepare armed forces for war.

monarchy state headed by a king, queen, emperor or empress.

nationalism exaggerated love of one's country.

naval blockade cutting off a country's supplies from the sea.

neutral not taking sides in a conflict.

parliamentary government government by the people's elected representatives.

partisanship taking sides.

partition dividing up.

propaganda political information (often false) that gives only one point of view. Like advertising, it is designed to influence the way people think.

protocol agreement or understanding that establishes how things are to be done or conducted.

province part of a country or empire.

reparation compensation paid for war damage.

republic country with an elected head of state.

revolution complete and swift uprising that causes some basic political changes.

surface ships all normal ships, as opposed to submarines.

terrorism war waged by individuals or small groups, usually with shootings and bombings.

terrorist a person engaged in terrorism.

Thrace European Turkey, to the west of the Bosporus.

treaty legal agreement between states.

tyrannical government or behaviour not bound by the law.

ultimatum final terms that usually cannot be rejected.

unification joining together.

Sources and Resources

Further Reading
J. Brooman, *The End of Old Europe: The Causes of the First World War, 1914-18*, Longman, 1985.

Graham Darby, *Origins of the First World War*, Longman, 1998.

Stewart Ross, *Assassination in Sarajevo: the Trigger for World War I*, Heinemann, 2001.

D.G. Williamson, *War and Peace: International Relations 1914-1945*, Longman, 1994.

Other Sources
Norman Angell, *The Great Illusion*, Heinemann, 1909.

H.H. Asquith, *The Genesis of War*, Cassell, 1923.

Barry Bates, *The First World War*, Blackwell, 1984.

C.W. Boyd, ed., *Mr Chamberlain's Speeches*, 2 vols, Constable, 1914.

F.R. Bridge, *The Coming of the First World War*, 1983.

Grey, Viscount E., *Twenty-five Years, 1892-1916*, 2 vols, Hodder & Stoughton, 1925.

Ruth Henig, *The Origins of the First World War*, Routledge, 1993.

Richard Hofstadter, *Great Issues in American History*, 2 vols, Vintage, New York, 1958.

Alistair Horne, *The Fall of Paris*, Macmillan, London, 1965.

Michael Hurst, *Key Treaties for the Great Powers, 1814-1914*, 2 vols, David & Charles, 1974.

J. Joll, *The Origins of the First World War*, 1984.

D. Kennedy, *The Rise and Fall of the Great Powers*, 1988.

Laurence Lafore, *The Long Fuse: An Interpretation of the Origins of World War I*, Waveland, 1997.

Gordon Martel, *The Origins of the First World War*, Longman, 1987.

Steven E. Miller, Sean M. Lynn-Jones, Stephen Van Evera, *Military Strategy and the Origins of the First World War*, Princeton, 1991.

Stewart Ross, *Admiral Sir Francis Bridgeman*, Baily's, 1998.

Stewart Ross, *Causes and Consequences of the First World War*, Evans, 1997.

A.J. Stevenson, *The First World War and International Politics*, 1991.

Hew Strachan, *The First World War. Vol. I: To Arms*, Oxford University Press, 2001.

A.J.P. Taylor, *The Struggle for the Mastery of Europe*, Oxford University Press, 1991.

Barbara Tuchman, *The Zimmermann Telegram*, Ballantine, 1985.

Websites
There are many websites containing information on the First World War. These are good places to start your search:

http://www.pvhs.chico.k12.ca.us/~bsilva/projects/great_war/causes.htm

http://www.schoolshistory.org.uk/firstworldwar.htm

http://mars.acnet.wnec.edu/~grempel/courses/wc2/lectures/worldwar1.html

http://www.lib.msu.edu/sowards/balkan/lect15.htm

Places to Visit:
The Imperial War Museum
Lambeth Road
London SE1 6HZ
Tel: 020 7416 5000

Index

If a number is in **bold** type, there is an illustration.

Aehrenthal, Alois von 34, 35, 36
Africa 9, 13, 18, 39, 52, 53
Albania 30, 40, 43
Alexander II, Tsar (Russia) 11
Algeçiras Conference 20, 22, 23, 24
Alsace and Lorraine 5, 24, 29
Anglo-Japanese Alliance 19
Anglo-Russian entente 26, 27, 29
Arab Revolt 52
Austria-Hungary 6, 7, 9, 10, 14, 15, 40, 43
  alliances 11, 12, 27, 33, 36, 37, 46
  declares war 48
  empire 6, 9, 30, 31, 34, 35, 36, 41, 44, 46
  military planning 34, 39, 41, 42, 46
  ultimatum to Serbia 47, 48

Balkans 9, 12, 13, 17, 30, 31, 35, 36, **40**, 41, 42, 46, 48, 54
Belgium 13, 24, 25, 50, 51
Berlin-Baghdad Railway **23**
Bethmann Hollweg, Theobald von **46**, 50
Bismarck, Otto von 4, 10, **11**, 12, **13**, **14**, 27
Black Hand Gang 44, 45, 46
Bosnia-Herzegovina 30, 31, 34, 35, 36, 37, 44, 45, 46
Boxer Rebellion 18, **19**
Britain 7, 9, 10, 16
  alliances 10, 15, 16, 17, 18, 19, 20, 23, 25, 26, 27, 36, 50, 52, 54
  army 23, 33, 52, 53
  declares war 50
  empire 7, 10, 13, 18, 20, 26, 29, 30, 31, **32**, 53
  industry 7, 8, 31
  military planning 23, 27, 33, 38, 39, 42
  navy 7, 16, 17, 23, 24, 33, 37, 38, 39, 46, 53, 54, 56
  'splendid isolation' 16, 17, 19
  trade 7, 32
British Expeditionary Force (BEF) 23
Bulgaria 30, 40, 54

China 18, 19, 20, 21, 52
Conrad, Franz von 34, 35, 39, 41, 42

Dardanelles 52, 53

Delcassé, Théophile 20, 22
Dreadnought, HMS **24**
Dual Alliance 11, 12, 33, 36
Dual Entente 14, 15, 17

Edward VII, King (Britain) **20**
Entente Cordiale 20, 23, 29

France 4, 5, 7, 10, 12, 48
  alliances 11, 14, 15, 18, 19, 20, 22, 23, 24, 25, 27, 36, 47
  army **33**, 50, 52
  empire 7, 13, 18, 20, 22, 37
  navy 12, 33, 54
  war with Prussia 4, 5, 7, 17
Franz Ferdinand, Archduke **44**, 45, 46, 58
Franz Josif I, Emperor (Austria) 11, 44, 46

German East Africa 52, 53
Germany 4, 5, 6, 7, 9, 10, 13, 15
  alliances 11, 12, 14, 17, 19, 21, 27, 33, 36, 39, **46**
  army 17, 33, 49, **50**, 53
  'blank cheque' 46, 47
  declares war 49, 50, 59
  empire 6, 7, 13, 18, 22, 29, 38, 52
  industry **7**, 8, 32
  military planning 24, 25, 38, 39, 42, 48, 50, 51
  navy 16, 17, 24, 32, 33, 37, 39, 46, 56
  U-boat campaign **42**, 56, 57
  unification 4, 5
Greece 30, 40, 54
Grey, Sir Edward **26**, 33, 43, 50

Haldane, Lord **39**

imperialism 9, 10, 13, 18, 29, 30, 31
India 7, 10, 30, **32**
Italy 7, 8, 10, 12, 15, 18, 24, 27, 33, 39, 51, **54**
Izvolsky, A.P. 26, **36**

Japan 9, 10, 15, 19, **21**, 24, 29, 51, 52, 57

League of the Three Emperors 11, 12
Libya 39, 54
Lloyd George, David **38**
Lusitania 56, **57**

Monroe Doctrine **9**, 54
Montenegro 30, 40, 51
Morocco 20, 22, 23, 29, 37, 38

Napoleon III, Emperor (France) 4
nationalism 28, 29, 31, 43, 44, 58
Nicholas II, Tsar (Russia) **15**, 21
Ottoman Empire *see* Turkey

Panslavism 35
Panther **37**
Princip, Gavrilo **45**
Prussia 4, 5

Reinsurance Treaty 12, 14
religion 18, 19, 30, 31
Romania 30, 40, 54
Russia 6, 7, 8, 9, 10, 13, 40
  alliances 11, 12, 14, 15, 18, 19, 21, 22, 25, 26, 27, 35, 36, 46, 47
  army 21, 33, **42**, **47**, **48**, 49
  empire 6, 9, 15, 18, 26, 29, 31
  industry 8, 25
  navy 21, 36
Russian Revolution (1905) 21, 26
Russo-Japanese War 10, 15, **21**, 22, 26, 29

Sarajevo **44**, 45, 51, 58
Schlieffen, Alfred von 24, **25**
Schlieffen Plan 24, 25, 48, 50
Scramble for Africa **13**, 39
Serbia 30, 31, 35, 36, 40, 41, 43, 44, 46, 47, 48, 51, 59
South Africa 7, 16, 19, 29
Spain 20, 22
Suez Canal **30**

Treaty of Frankfurt 5
Treaty of London 40, 50, 51, 54
Treaty of Versailles 58, **59**
Triple Alliance **12**, 15, 17, 19, 20, 24, 27, 33, 54
Triple Entente 27, 29, 33
Turkey 6, 7, 9, 10, 13, 14, 51, 52
  empire 6, 9, 23, 28, 30, 31, 34, 35, 39, 40, 43

USA 6, 9, 17, 24, 29, 31, 32, 52, 54, 55, 56, 57

Victoria, Queen (Britain) **10**, **12**, 14

Wilhelm I, Emperor (Germany) 5, 11
Wilhelm II, Emperor (Germany) 10, **14**, 16, 17, 20, 21, **22**, 23, 27, 29, 42, 46, 47
Wilson, Woodrow 54, **55**, 57, **59**

Zimmermann, Arthur 57